FINDING OUT ABOUT HOLIDAYS

Valentine's Day

Candy, Love, and Hearts

Elaine Landau

Enslow Publishers, Inc.

40 Industrial Road   PO Box 38
Box 398   Aldershot
Berkeley Heights, NJ 07922   Hants GU12 6BP
USA   UK

http://www.enslow.com

For Emily Garmizo

Library of Congress Cataloging-in-Publication Data

Landau, Elaine.
  Valentine's day—candy, love, and hearts / Elaine Landau.
    p. cm. — (Finding out about holidays)
  Includes bibliographical references and index.
  ISBN 0-7660-1779-6
  1. Valentine's Day—United States—Juvenile literature. I. Title. II. Series.
  GT4925.L36 2002
  394.2618'0973—dc21
                     2001000989

Printed in the United States of America

10 9 8 7 6 5 4 3 2

To Our Readers: We have done our best to make sure all Internet addresses in this book were active and appropriate when we went to press. However, the author and the publisher have no control over and assume no liability for the material available on those Internet sites or on other Web sites they may link to. Any comments or suggestions can be sent by e-mail to comments@enslow.com or to the address on the back cover.

Every effort has been made to locate all copyright holders of material used in this book. If any errors or omissions have occurred, corrections will be made in future editions of this book.

Photo Credits: AP Photo / The Gazette, Mark Christian, p. 25; Cameramann International, Ltd., pp. 17, 38; Cheryl Wells, p. 43; COMPUSERVE/Associated Press, p. 30 (both); © Corel Corporation, pp. 5 (both), 6, 7 (bottom), 20, 24, 26, 29, 32, 33, 41 (all), 42 (backgound), 43 (background), 44, 46, 47, 48; Hemera Technologies, pp. i, ii, iii, 7 (top), 9, 13, 15, 21, 27, 34, 37 (both), 39, 40 (both); Historical Pictures Services, Chicago, p. 12; Courtesy of www.valentine-ne.com, p. 35; Hulton Getty Collection/Archive Photos, pp. 16, 18, 19; Jim Tuten /Associated Press, p. 28; Joan Slatkin/Archive Photos, pp. 22, 45; Kevin Higley/Associated Press, p. 36; Lambert/Archive Photos, pp. 8, 23; Michael Schulman Archive/Archive Photos, p. 4; Saint Valentine, Gift of Joanne Freedman, Photograph © 2001 Board of Trustees, National Gallery of Art, Washington, p. 11; Sakchai Lalit/Associated Press, p. 31; William Sauts Bock, pp. 10, 14.

Cover Credits: © Corel Corporation (background and middle inset); Joan Slatkin/Archive Photos (top inset); Hulton Getty/Archive Photos (bottom inset).

CONTENTS

Giving Valentine's Day gifts and cards is a fun way to let your family and friends know that you care about them!

CHAPTER 1

Cards, Cards, Cards

It is fun to give cards to all your friends and family on Valentine's Day. You can buy cards at the store, but it is even more fun to make your own!

Many people like to send greeting cards. There are cards for birthdays, weddings, and school graduations. Cards bring good wishes and show that we care.

Cards are also often sent on holidays. Millions of Christmas cards are mailed each year. Halloween cards are always fun to send. But we do not give cards on every holiday. Usually, cards are not sent on holidays such as Columbus Day, Washington's Birthday, or Martin Luther King, Jr. Day.

Yet there is one holiday especially known for

May time deal gently with you

To my true Valentine

To My Valentine

Pink roses all made in a Heart,
Thoughts of modesty do impart.
Fair maid it is all thine
Will you be my Valentine.

Some valentines, like the old-fashioned one pictured here, have words about love and friendship written on them.

cards. These cards have words about love or friendship. Often they are red or pink. Some have hearts on them. They are called valentines. Many people make their own valentines. Other people buy them in stores.

You can give a valentine card to anyone you care about. Children may give them to friends.

Parents may give them to their children. Grandparents may give them to their grandchildren. Some people even give their pets valentines.

People send valentine cards each year on February 14, Valentine's Day. It is not the same kind of holiday as Presidents' Day. Schools are open on Valentine's Day. So are banks and businesses. Mail carriers are especially busy that day. They deliver tons of valentines.

Valentine's Day is a special time. It is a day for friendship and caring. It is a holiday about love.

Valentine's Day is all about friendship and love.

Skywriters can remind everyone that it is Valentine's Day.

CHAPTER 2

How It All Began

ROMAN ORIGINS

★

Valentine's Day is believed to have come from the time of the ancient Romans. Each year on February 15, the Romans would have a big festival to honor the god Lupercus, who was thought to protect everyone from wolves.

Valentine's Day is not a new holiday. People have celebrated it for hundreds of years. Yet no one is sure exactly how Valentine's Day started.

It may have started with the ancient Romans. They lived over 2,000 years ago in the country of Italy. Each year on February 15, they held a special celebration known as the festival of Lupercalia. The festival honored the Roman god Lupercus. The Romans believed that Lupercus protected them from wolves.

Everyone enjoyed the festival. People danced

There are several stories that explain how Valentine's Day began. But most of them seem to have come from ancient Rome.

and sang. There were footraces and people played games for hours.

One game was a way for young people to meet. It began the night before the festival. On the evening of February 14, the girls gathered

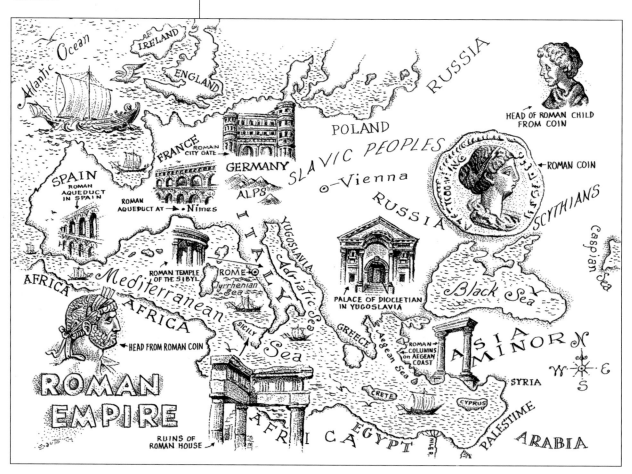

together. They wrote their names on pieces of paper. The papers were put into a large bowl.

Each boy picked a paper from the bowl. He could not peek at the name on it. The girl whose name he picked would be his partner during the festival. All the couples spent the day together. Some fell in love and later married.

Many people believe that Valentine's Day started differently. They think it may have started with two priests. Both men were named Valentine.

One story also takes place in ancient Rome in the third century A.D. Claudius II, the emperor, was a cruel ruler. He wanted Christians to give up their religion. He told them to pray to the Roman gods. Those who refused were jailed or even killed.

Nobody knows for sure what Saint Valentine looked like. Here is one idea of how he may have looked.

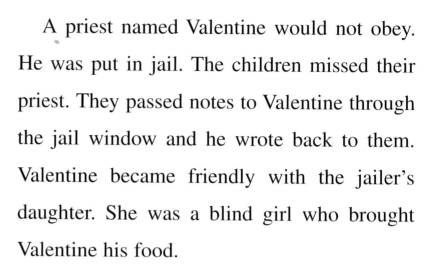

Here is yet another artist's idea of how Saint Valentine may have looked.

A priest named Valentine would not obey. He was put in jail. The children missed their priest. They passed notes to Valentine through the jail window and he wrote back to them. Valentine became friendly with the jailer's daughter. She was a blind girl who brought Valentine his food.

Even in jail, Valentine was not safe from Claudius II. The emperor again ordered Valentine to pray to the Roman gods. The priest refused, and he was killed on February 14.

Valentine wrote one last note to the jailer's daughter before he died. According to the story, the blind girl was able to read the note. She could see again. The priest wrote on the note: "From Your Valentine." Some say that is why we send valentine cards today.

But is it? There is also a story about another priest named Valentine. He also stood up to Emperor Claudius II, but for a different reason.

Claudius II had wanted to build a powerful army. He ordered his soldiers not to marry. The emperor did not want the men to think about their families. He wanted them to think only about winning battles.

Claudius II warned priests not to marry people. But Valentine did not listen. He married young couples anyway, and was arrested. Claudius II had him killed on February 14.

Some people think both stories are true. But they believe the stories are about the same man. Was there only one Valentine? We may never know.

Claudius would not allow his soldiers to get married.

Valentine would not pray to Roman gods, such as Mars, the god of war.

Perhaps one priest named Valentine did many good things. Maybe he refused to pray to the Roman gods. He also may have helped young lovers to marry. And he could have been a friend to children. Valentine was later made a saint.

But wait, the story is not over. There is still another tale about how Valentine's Day may have started. This one began long ago in England. People there noticed that many birds picked their mates around February 14. They felt that people should do the same. So February 14 became a day for love.

Which Valentine's Day story is true? In

some ways they may all be. Boys picked girls' names out of a bowl during Lupercalia. Today, schoolchildren do something like that. At parties they often pick valentines out of a box.

A priest named Valentine sent kind notes. Now people send Valentine's Day cards. Birds are still a part of Valentine's Day, too. Lovebirds make us think of love. They are often seen on Valentine's Day cards. Valentine's Day is probably a mix of many different stories and ideas.

It is fun to think about how Valentine's Day may have started. It is even more fun to celebrate it.

Lovebirds are often pictured on cards for Valentine's Day.

This is a valentine that was hand-made in the early 1900s, when sending valentines really became popular in America.

Let's Celebrate!

Valentine's Day is celebrated throughout the United States. Many people send cards. This idea began in America in the mid-1700s. Most of the early valentine cards were homemade.

Valentines really became popular in the early 1900s. By then, there were large greeting-card companies. People could buy nice cards at low prices. There were even penny Valentines. Children especially liked these. They gave them to their friends.

There was another reason valentine cards became popular. It had nothing to do with love

*"He loves me, or he loves me not?
The daisy petals say
"He loves – he loves, he loves
you dear,
Sweet Valentine to-day!"*

**Some Valentine's Day
cards have poems, like
the one shown here.**

or friendship. It was due to the mail service. In 1790, there were only about 75 post offices in the United States. By 1900, there were more than 75,000. More post offices made it easier to send valentines. People anywhere could receive them.

Today you can find all kinds of valentine cards. Some are even musical. When one of these is opened, a song plays. Some valentine cards are very large. They are so big they may not fit in the mailbox. The mail carrier might have to bring them directly to the door.

There are cards with long love poems. But there are short, funny valentines, too. Americans spend about $277 million on valentine cards every year. The only holiday that people spend more on cards is Christmas.

Hearts, cupids, and lovebirds are

Valentine's Day symbols. They stand for things that we think of on Valentine's Day. Hearts stand for the love people show on Valentine's Day. Cupid is the Roman god of love. He has wings and a bow and arrow. Cupid's arrow stands for love. Anyone hit by Cupid's arrow falls in love. Lovebirds stand

This Valentine's Day postcard shows Cupid, the Roman god of love, mending a broken heart.

Heart-shaped cookies are fun to make.

for romance. This goes along with the old belief that birds mate on February 14.

Often, schools have Valentine's Day celebrations. Students might decorate their classrooms. Many also make Valentine's Day cards. They might cut out hearts, cupids, and lovebirds. Usually red or pink paper is used. These are Valentine's Day colors.

Children often give one another valentine cards at school parties. Special Valentine's Day treats might also be served. There will probably be cookies in the shape of hearts. Cupcakes with pink icing, chocolates wrapped in red foil, and small heart-shaped sugar candies with Valentine's Day sayings on them are all popular treats.

Some schools and clubs have Valentine's Day dances. There are Valentine's Day fairs, too. At these, clowns do face painting. They might paint hearts and cupids on children's cheeks.

Valentine's Day games are fun. People might toss a heart-shaped beanbag or guess the

Some people make special Valentine's Day desserts, such as this heart-shaped cake.

Special treats, like these lollipops, are fun to give to friends and family.

number of pink-and-red jelly beans in a big jar. Valentine's Day foods are also always sold. The heart-shaped pizzas are delicious. There will be lots of pink-and-red desserts as well.

Most public libraries celebrate Valentine's Day. Often, the children's room is decorated for the holiday. Children's books about Valentine's Day are put on display. Sometimes special bookmarks are given out. These might list more books for holiday reading. Many libraries offer Valentine's Day programs. A children's theater group might perform. There might also be a Valentine's Day arts and crafts time.

But not only children celebrate Valentine's

Day. Adults enjoy cards and candy, too. Millions of heart-shaped boxes of chocolate are given. Often, flowers are also sent.

Some children give their parents "helpful" Valentines. These are more than cards. They are also gifts. The children decorate paper hearts. On them, they write something they will do to help their parents. They might write: "This valentine is good for one week of dog walking." A week of dish washing is another good choice. Parents love getting these. So do grandparents. But helpful valentines can be for anyone.

Many young people try to make Valentine's Day extra special. They use the day to be a better friend or to do something kind.

You are never too young to give or get a valentine!

Many people, such as firefighters and police officers, work hard each day to keep us all safe. We should remember them on Valentine's Day, too!

They can also thank someone who was very nice.

Some students make valentines for people who might not get one. They may give a beautiful card to the school crossing guard. The janitor or school nurse might get one, too.

Sometimes a whole class might work on

one large valentine. It could be given to a local fire station. Firefighters and police officers protect the community. Valentine's Day is a day to show that we care. Class valentines can also go to children in a hospital. People in nursing homes like getting them, too. Valentine cards make everyone feel good.

Kindness has no limits. Valentine's Day is a good time to prove that.

Making cards for people in the hospital makes everyone feel good!

Thousands of couples get married each year on Valentine's Day.

CHAPTER 4

Valentine's Day Weddings

Valentine's Day has long been a day for love. It is also a day for weddings. Every year, thousands of couples get married on February 14.

Chapels across the country are very busy that day. Many couples flock to our nation's wedding capital. That is Las Vegas, Nevada.

There are over 50 wedding chapels in Las Vegas. On Valentine's Day, many are open around the clock. Some have a wedding every fifteen minutes. Often, Las Vegas Valentine's Day weddings are highly unusual.

One couple was married on a ship. The ship

HOW TO SAY "I LOVE YOU"

The words "I love you" can be said in so many different ways.

Spanish
Te amo

French
Je t'aime

German
Ich liebe Sie

Italian
Ti voglia bene

Portuguese
Eu te amo

Russian
Ya tebya liubliu

Greek
S'agapo

One Valentine's Day, 24 couples were married on a roller coaster at Busch Gardens in Florida. Shown here (from the left) is Matt Ledon and Melissa Williams, who were married on this ride, the Montu.

was docked in front of the Treasure Island Casino. A crew of sailors and pirates were on hand for the ceremony. Another couple was wed at the Harley-Davidson Café. After the ceremony, they hopped on their motorcycles. The bride and groom rode around the city to celebrate. In still another ceremony, the couple said their vows in a hot air balloon!

Some couples get married in a hot air balloon.

Can you imagine getting married over the Internet? Joseph Perling and Victoria Vaughn did!

A Las Vegas group wedding was held in a museum of wax figures. A number of couples were married at the same time. Wax figures were placed among the brides and grooms. These looked very real. It was hard to tell the wax figures from the real couples!

But unusual Valentine's Day weddings are not just in Las Vegas. Some people have

These couples were married in Bangrak, or "Love Place," in Bangkok, Thailand.

At military weddings, the bride and groom are saluted with swords.

actually gone to Thailand for this. One year, 36 couples had a group wedding there.

It was an underwater event. The couples wore wedding clothes over their diving gear. They exchanged rings beneath the sea. The brides and grooms signed waterproof marriage documents. They used special pens for this.

All these couples had unforgettable weddings. For them, Valentine's Day will always be extra special.

Couples in other countries get married on Valentine's Day, too. They dress in the clothing and colors that have special meaning for them.

Giving a sweetheart flowers is another way of celebrating Valentine's Day.

CHAPTER 5

Special Ways to Celebrate

E-MAIL VALENTINES

★

A fun way to send valentines is over the Internet. Many Web sites, such as the ones on page 47, offer cards that you can send for free.

In some places, whole towns celebrate Valentine's Day. That happens each year in Loveland, Colorado. Loveland's nickname is "The Sweetheart City." On Valentine's Day, the city lives up to its name and its nickname.

The fun starts at the Loveland post office. Valentines mailed through Loveland get special treatment. They are stamped with a short valentine poem.

Loveland's post office does even more for the holiday. It has a Valentine "re-mailing" program. People from around the world take part. They

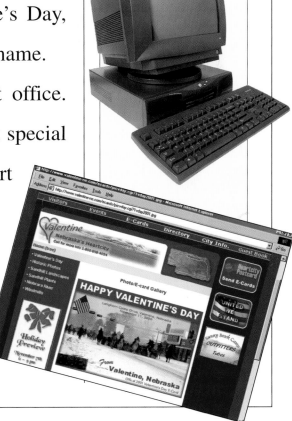

People all over the world mail their cards to a post office in Loveland, Colorado to be stamped with a special Valentine's Day poem. Here, postal worker C.J. Kilbourn works with valentines to get them mailed out on time.

send their valentines to the Loveland post office. The special stamp with the poem is added. Then the cards are sent on their way.

The town also has a holiday contest to pick a "Miss Loveland Valentine." She will be Miss Loveland Valentine for one year.

The winner is always a student from the

high school. The judges look for a special girl. She must have good grades. But personality is important, too.

Candy and flowers are popular gifts to give on Valentine's Day.

Miss Loveland Valentine is kept busy. She attends all the town's events. She even visits the state's governor.

Boys are not left out of the fun. Each year a young boy is picked to be Cowboy Cupid. He is usually between four and six years old. Cowboy Cupid also goes to town celebrations. He is never hard to spot. He wears a cowboy outfit and, like Cupid, he carries a bow and arrow.

The town is also decorated in pink and red

for the holiday. Businesses hang hearts or cupids outside their buildings. Valentine's Day cards are hung between lampposts.

Other towns celebrate in a big way, too. That is true of Valentine, Nebraska. It is known as America's "Heart City." Each year the Heart

In many schools, children make their own valentines in class.

City has special Valentine celebrations. One is the Valentine's Day Coronation. At real coronations, kings and queens are crowned. Valentine, Nebraska, crowns a king and queen of hearts.

Everyone knows the royal couple. They are students from Valentine's Rural High School. Their classmates vote to choose them. They also vote for members of the Royal Valentine Court. This includes a prince and princess of hearts. There is a duke and duchess of hearts as well.

Valentine, Nebraska, has held the coronation for over 55 years. It is always on the Sunday before Valentine's Day. Many people come to see the event. The high school band plays music. Students sing. High school students have a dance.

Roses are popular flowers on Valentine's Day.

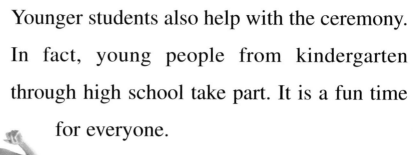

In some schools and towns, there are special dances on Valentine's Day.

Younger students also help with the ceremony. In fact, young people from kindergarten through high school take part. It is a fun time for everyone.

The Heart City has other celebrations as well. These are not all for young people. At the Sweetheart Festival, couples married for fifty or more years are honored. A senior Valentine king and queen are crowned. In America's Heart City, Valentine's Day is for people of all ages.

Valentine's Day may be extra special in Valentine, Nebraska. The same goes for Loveland, Colorado. But this holiday can be terrific anywhere. It is a day for love and friendship. These are things for people everywhere to share.

We should show others we love them every day, not just on Valentine's Day.

41

Valentine's Day Craft Project

★

Heart People

You can make Valentine's Day special by doing more than sending cards. Try making these fun heart-shaped people to give out to loved ones or to decorate with. You will need:

- ✔ **2 sheets red construction paper**
- ✔ **2 sheets pink construction paper**
- ✔ **1 sheet white construction paper**
- ✔ **15 small assorted hearts**
- ✔ **white glue**
- ✔ **safety scissors**

1. Cut out two large hearts: one pink and one red.

2. Cut out four small hearts: two pink and two red.

3. Glue the bottom of the large red heart to the bottom of the large pink heart.

4. Cut the white paper into four 2½" by 10" strips.

5. Fold each strip back and forth, like an accordion.

6. Glue the small red hearts to two of the white strips. Glue the small pink hearts to the other two strips.

7. Attach the strips to the body (made up of the two large hearts) to make arms and legs. Arrange the small hearts to make a face. Glue these pieces together.

8. Let your heart person dry for 15 minutes, then display it for everyone to see!

*Safety Note: Be sure to ask for help from an adult, if needed, to complete this project.

Valentine's Day Craft Project

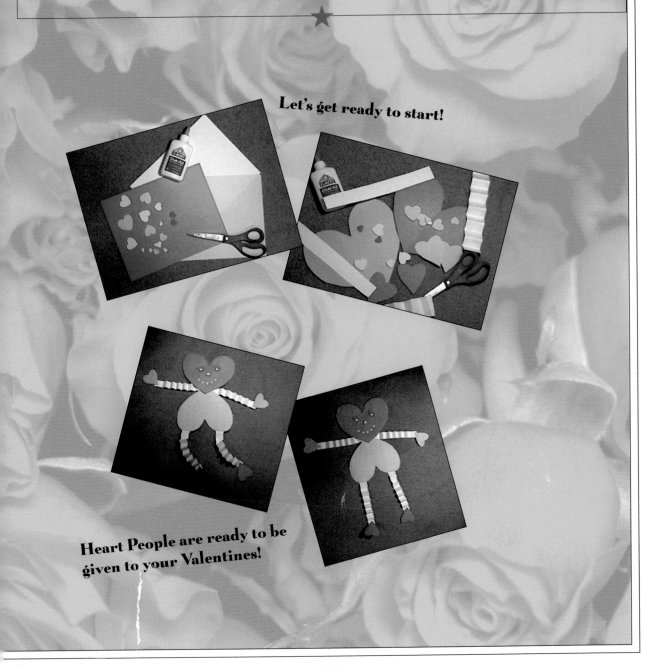

Let's get ready to start!

Heart People are ready to be given to your Valentines!

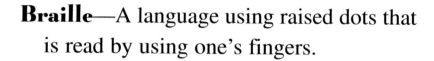
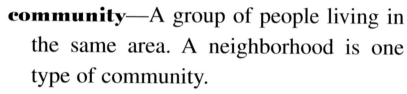
Braille—A language using raised dots that is read by using one's fingers.

community—A group of people living in the same area. A neighborhood is one type of community.

Claudius II—A Roman emperor who ruled during the third century A.D.

Cupid—The Roman god of love.

Lupercalia—An ancient Roman festival.

Words to Know

★

penny Valentines—Valentine's Day cards that cost one cent.

popular—Well liked.

symbol—Something that stands for something else.

Valentine—The Roman priest who was made a saint. Valentine's Day is named after him. A valentine can also be a card given on Valentine's Day.

Reading About

Bulla, Clyde Robert, *The Story of Valentine's Day*. New York: Harper Collins, 1999.

Burke, Susan Slatterly, *My Very Own Valentine's Day: A Book of Cooking and Crafts*. Minneapolis, Minn.: The Lerner Publishing Group, 1993.

Roop, Connie. *Let's Celebrate Valentine's Day!* Brookfield, Conn.: Millbrook Press, 1999.

Ross, Kathy. *Crafts for Valentine's Day*. Brookfield, Conn.: Millbrook Press, 1995.

Supraner, Robyn. *Valentine's Day: Things to Make and Do*. Mahwah, N.J.: Troll Communications L.L.C., 1997.

Internet Addresses

★

VALENTINE FUN AT KIDS DOMAIN
http://www.kidsdomain.com/holiday/val/
    index.html

VALENTINE, NEBRASKA E-CARDS
http://heartcity.net/ecards

Index

THE PARISIAN SENSATION
VALENTINE

Words by ALBERT WILL
Music by CHRISTI
American Version by HERBERT